Annette Cornell

SINGLES *who* FLOURISH

21 DAY DEVOTIONAL
ON CONNECTING YOUR HEART TO CHRIST

TRILOGY
A WHOLLY OWNED SUBSIDIARY OF TBN
PROFESSIONAL PUBLISHING MEETS POWERFUL PROMOTION

Trilogy Christian Publishers
A Wholly Owned Subsidiary of Trinity Broadcasting Network
2442 Michelle Drive
Tustin, CA 92780
Copyright © 2024 by Annette Cornell
Scripture quotations marked (KJV) taken from *The Holy Bible, King James Version*. Cambridge Edition: 1769.
Scripture quotations marked NLT are taken from the Holy Bible, New Living Translation, copyright © 1996, 2004, 2015 by Tyndale House Foundation. Used by permission of Tyndale House Publishers, Inc., Carol Stream, Illinois 60188. All rights reserved.
Scripture quotations marked AMP are taken from the Amplified® Bible (AMP), Copyright © 2015 by The Lockman Foundation. Used by permission. www.Lockman.org.
Scripture quotations marked ERV are taken from the Easy-to-Read Version®. Copyright © 2006 by Bible League international. Public domain.

All rights reserved, including the right to reproduce this book or portions thereof in any form whatsoever.
For information, address Trilogy Christian Publishing
Rights Department, 2442 Michelle Drive, Tustin, CA 92780.
Trilogy Christian Publishing/ TBN and colophon are trademarks of Trinity Broadcasting Network.
For information about special discounts for bulk purchases, please contact Trilogy Christian Publishing.

Trilogy Disclaimer: The views and content expressed in this book are those of the author and may not necessarily reflect the views and doctrine of Trilogy Christian Publishing or the Trinity Broadcasting Network.

10 9 8 7 6 5 4 3 2 1
Library of Congress Cataloging-in-Publication Data is available.
ISBN 979-8-89333-319-0
ISBN 979-8-89333-320-6 (ebook)

INTRODUCTION

I must have written this intro a bunch of times. I wanted this to be perfect. Almost like my life. Without any mistakes or blemishes. Well, at least none that are visible to the outer world. But there's something that I learned that recently made me realize that whatever I do, whoever I am, does not need to be perfect. I am perfected through Christ. I know it sounds so cliché, but it is the truth.

Earlier this year I finally decided to take my singleness journey more seriously and share my progress with the world. This journey was to help me get to a great place of healing, happiness, and wholeness. Most importantly, this journey was to help me connect my heart to Christ. In February 2019, I made a declaration to the Lord that I would remain single to focus on myself and my relationship with Him. I wanted the Lord to bring the person whom He wanted me to be in a relationship with and prepare me for when this partner comes. I also knew that throughout the past few years, my heart had taken some bruising and scarring that only the Lord could see and heal. Maybe you can relate to being fed up and making a similar declaration to Christ?

I was at a point in my life where I was in desperate need of spiritual guidance and unconditional love that I knew I could only get from the Lord. I was not in a good place when it came to my finances, career, or connections. I was tired of struggling financially and knew that all these things were connected. I no longer wanted to handle things on my own, as I have been doing in the past. It obviously was not working the way I wanted it to. February 2019 was when I decided to get out of the driver's seat and trust the Lord to take over the wheel. I was finally allowing God to guide me to the destination that He had for me. I was finally allowing God all the way inside of my heart to do some reconstruction.

I really believed that the end goal was for me to meet the love of my life and develop a great long-lasting relationship. And this did happen, just not with the person I was expecting it to happen with. I realized that the man I was looking for already found me. He was just waiting on me to open my heart and allow Him all the way in. Needless to say, I found God, and my relationship with Him grew intimate.

Have you experienced this? True intimacy. I mean someone who knows everything about you and still loves you unconditionally. I'm talking flaws, mistakes, shortcomings, insecurities, the things that you would not want anyone to know. If a person found out these things, would they still be there? Would they still love you? Because I know someone who would, and his name is Jesus. His love is unmatched: "Nor height, nor depth, nor any other creature, shall be able to separate us from the love of God, which is in Christ Jesus our Lord" (Romans 8:39, KJV).

Once my relationship with the Lord developed, I realized that I no longer cared about finding a man or getting into a relationship. That wasn't the end goal for me. Don't get me wrong, I'm not against being in a relationship and would love to meet that special person, but only if it's God's will for my life. See, that's the thing. I went into this season not knowing what to expect, and in the end, I found acceptance, joy, peace, happiness, love of the Father and love of myself. His love is healing. This is greater than anything I could have ever expected.

This devotional is compiled of twenty-one notes that I have written and shared with my blog throughout 2023. My intention in writing these notes was to record my singleness journey for other singles and whoever was interested in tracking my progress. I was not planning on releasing it to the entire world, but I know that this will help bless other singles who are struggling in their singleness season. My prayer is that you entrust your journey to the Lord, as I did. Let go of what you think you want and allow God to give you what and who you need. Open your heart and allow God in. He is the greatest heart surgeon who can fill every void and heal every scar. Even the ones that you don't even know are there.

If you are struggling with being single and find yourself impatient or in desperate need for someone to like you or be with you, this devotional is for you. If you don't feel complete, don't feel good enough, or are constantly comparing your life to those around you, this devotional is for you. If you feel like something is missing within your heart or find yourself constantly using people, places, or things to make you feel whole, this devotional is for you. If you have been having issues connecting with Christ, this devotional is for you. My prayer is that as you read each note, you will learn the kind of love you're looking for. That one-of-a-kind love is found within the Lord. Romans 5:8 (NLT) says, "But God showed his great love for us by sending Christ to die for us while we were still sinners."

I wasn't familiar with what a singleness journey consisted of, but I knew I needed three things: I needed to heal, grow, and flourish. In this devotional, you will see the evolution of my heart and mind. You will see my heart healing in real time. You will see my mind growing in knowledge of the word. You will see my relationship with God growing more intimate in real time. You will see the transformation of how God was leading me to a destination I did not expect. You will see the love of Christ flourishing in me.

Singleness was such a strange topic for me. I have never put focus on this season because I was always busy. Busy living, busy working, busy trying to be chosen. I didn't understand the importance of my singleness season. One might even say that I was overlooking a lot of important things. In this season, I was able to learn so much about myself and my God. I was able to remove all the distractions and focus on what made my life feel complete and happy. I was able to realize that I did not need to do anything extra to be chosen because someone had already chosen me. This being the Lord, my Father in Heaven, Jesus Christ. Connecting with Him changed my entire life, and for that, I am hoping that reading this devotional will change your life also. I'm hoping that you are able to develop a real relationship with the Lord and experience the fullness of His love. Let His love be the blueprint to any future relationships you experience.

2023: MOVING FORWARD

APRIL 2, 2023

Annette Visions

I took a little hiatus to allow God to work on my mind and heart. There were things that I needed clarity on.

I have been praying on this and decided to start back with my blogging. It has helped me tremendously to empty my feelings and thoughts onto this screen. And I'm hoping that these weekly posts will continue to help others, specifically my single ladies.

I have been on this singleness journey and have experienced some great times and not-so-great times. I would like to share this with you. Maybe you can relate. Maybe you just want to take this journey with me. Who knows where it will lead you and me?

I just thought it would be great to allow you to continue

to glimpse my vision of my world. Also, you can see all that God has done and is doing in my life. This is my testimony.

Are you ready to go on this singleness journey with me?

SINGLES WHO FLOURISH (NOTE 1)
APRIL 3, 2023
Annette Visions

Going through this singleness season has been rough, and let me tell you why. I have been so used to being in control, but I know that in order for God to work on my heart and mind, I will need to give them both completely to Him. This means me completely trusting in God.

How can I do this? How can a person who has felt the need to be in control release the reins? I can tell you three things that have helped to loosen the hold more and more. Maybe they can help you as well.

1. Doing things my way has not gotten me anywhere.
2. God knows and wants what is best for me.

3. What is the worst that can happen?

I say "loosen the hold" because I can't lie and say that my trust is 100% in the Lord right now, but I will say I'm 95% there. And I'm so grateful for this. I just don't have the capacity to worry or be afraid about where I will end up and who I will end up with. I can't worry about my age, my fertility, how others view me, what others my age have or are doing, or lastly whether I am losing out on something good because of the timing.

God has got me covered, and He will bring me someone good. How do I know? I'm reminded of this anytime I read Psalm☐

If it's not here yet, that just means that it is on the way, or shall I say, "my person, my man, my king, my husband, my handsome face, my helpmate, my love" is on the way, and he will be better than anyone that I could ever ask for or imagine. And this I am certain about!

SINGLES WHO FLOURISH (NOTE 2)
APRIL 6, 2023
Annette Visions

Lately, this one Scripture has been on my mind:

"Promise me, O women of Jerusalem, not to awaken love until the time is right." (Song of Songs)

I feel like a lot of times when you get weary being single for a long period of time, the normal reaction is to want to rush into a relationship. You no longer want to wait on God, but instead, you will try to make things happen on your own. That may even mean lowering your standards or being okay with things that you know are less than what you deserve. All the while, your mind is going a mile a minute doubting the promise that God made to you.

"And the Lord God caused a deep sleep to

fall upon Adam, and he slept: and he took one of his ribs, and closed up the flesh instead thereof; and the rib, which the Lord God had taken from man, made he a woman, and brought her unto the man." (Genesis 2:21–22, KJV)

God put Adam in a deep sleep to take a rib from him to create Eve. Have you ever stopped to think that maybe your person is probably in a deep sleep so God can work on him AND you? Have you thought that maybe that's the delay? God is taking His time to mold both of your minds and hearts.

I don't know if you're familiar with surgery, but that's not a one-two-three thing. It takes time and precision in order for it to be successful, especially when you're taking a part of one person and putting it in another. Not to mention the recovery or healing process afterward. Ask anyone in the medical field if you don't believe me.

Who had God being the surgeon, anesthesiologist, and nurse when it comes to relationship surgery on their bingo card? Because that's exactly what He does. God is able to do all of this while both you and your "Adam" are living your lives, navigating this singleness journey. But just like after every surgery, the patient is eventually awakened and on the path to a new and improved life. That is with some healing and recovery time, of course.

1. Trust God's timing. Only He will know when you

both are ready.

2. Continue to heal your mind, body, and soul. You want to make sure everything functions correctly so you can feel complete and whole.

3. You should not awaken love before it is ready. Wait on God. Let Him be the one to bring your "Adam" out of that deep sleep and straight to you.

God's introduction will be way better than anything you could ever imagine, and you and your "Adam" will be in way better shape mentally, physically, emotionally, spiritually, and financially when you both join together.

SINGLES WHO FLOURISH (NOTE 3)

APRIL 10, 2023

Annette Visions

I want you to do something for me ... I want you to answer the following questions honestly. You can either say them out loud to yourself, write them down in your notes, or answer them in your mind. You ready?

1. Do you feel that you are more precious or valuable than rubies?

2. Are you trustworthy? Can you add value to a man's life?

3. Do you attract positivity, or do you prefer drama?

4. Do you work or have any hobbies that you are passionate about?

5. Do you wake up early to take care of business and

run errands, or do you prefer to sleep in late?

6. Are you financially stable enough to provide and maintain the kind of lifestyle you are looking for in a man?

7. Would you consider yourself a hard worker?

8. Do you mind working overtime to obtain the things that you want?

9. Can a man put something in your possession and you increase the value by double or triple?

10. Do you give back to your community or people less fortunate?

11. Do you stick it out through the rough times?

12. Are you willing to do what's necessary to overcome obstacles?

13. Do you dress with grace and style?

14. Can you handle being with a man who is well known or of high importance? Can you fit into his world?

15. Are you willing to contribute to a man's calling or purpose?

16. Do you exhibit strength and dignity, and do you have no fear of the future?

17. Do you consider the things you say wise and kind, or are you controlling?

18. Are you focused on yourself and making sure that you get better daily, or are you focused on what everyone else has going on?

19. Are you a blessing to others?

20. Do you get compliments for being a great person or doing nice things for others?

21. Do you feel that you are one of a kind?

22. Do you fear the Lord?

Welp, if you made it to the end of this list and you were able to agree with most of these questions, then I would like to tell you, "Congratulations, Proverbs 31 woman! You are on your way to becoming a great wife."

I know what you're thinking: "Wife? How can I be a wife if I don't even have a boyfriend?" Well, let me tell you. Being a wife has more to do with your characteristics than the actual title. Any woman can get married, but embodying the role of a wife is a different story. It happens long before the wedding and the relationship.

Proverbs 31:10–31 does a great job of explaining the wife of a noble character. In this case, we can consider the "noble character" a king or a godly man who is happy, healthy, and whole.

If you possess these characteristics, then I am so happy for you. I felt the same way when I realized that I was finally living this Bible passage. I've always heard people talk about the Proverbs 31 woman, but it wasn't until I embarked on my singleness journey to becoming happy, healthy, and whole that I understood what this Bible passage meant.

I want to leave you with this: One day soon you will reap the rewards that all of your hard work has brought you and meet your king. That's what a healthy relationship will do for you. It will bring you favor from God beyond your imagination. I'm excited about this. Are you?

*Please read Proverbs 31:10–31 whenever you get a chance.

SINGLES WHO FLOURISH (NOTE 4)
APRIL 13, 2023
Annette Visions

Okay, so, I want to confirm something with you …

Please tell me when was the last time you saw a home or building that was built without a sturdy base. What happens to anything that is built on sand vs. rock? Would you agree that you need something solid to build upon? Well, I'm here to tell you that God is the solid foundation.

There is no way you can have a successful relationship without a solid relationship with God. He is the foundation and the blueprint. He is the contractor. God is the one who will bring you discipline, patience, love, joy, peace, gentleness, and understanding. He will shift your heart and mind so that the things you were once insecure about, you will now find confidence in. He will heal you and bless you with all that you need.

Just like in construction, God will work from the inside out, making sure that He covers every little detail to produce an amazing finished product. The finished product being a healthy, happy, and whole individual. And don't worry, God will stick with you from start to finish to be sure that you are completed perfectly and at the right time.

Will you hire God to be your contractor? Will you allow Him to work on you? The choice is yours. Just know that I'm happy with my results and would recommend, 10 out of 10.

> *"And I am certain that God, who began the good work within you, will continue his work until it is finally finished on the day when Christ Jesus returns." (Philippians 1:6, NLT)*

SINGLES WHO FLOURISH (NOTE 5)
APRIL 18, 2023
Annette Visions

I want to share something with you …

In my past, I made a lot of mistakes. I didn't always treat myself the best. I didn't always think of myself in a great light, and it reflected a lot in my friendships and relationships.

They say that you are supposed to teach others how to treat you by how you treat yourself, but honestly, there's something even greater that I have just recently come to understand: You should treat yourself how God treats you. You should see yourself how God sees you. You should not accept anything less from yourself, or from anyone else, than what the Lord has or will do for you.

Now, this is a great standard to live by, and let me

SINGLES WHO FLOURISH (NOTE 6)
APRIL 19, 2023
Annette Visions

I used to be one of those women who believed that there weren't a lot of men in this world. Women clearly outnumber men by a lot. I thought that the odds of getting into a relationship and finding a great guy to marry were very slim. I used to think that the only way this would be possible was if I jumped through hoops or traveled far in order to meet someone. But boy, was I wrong.

I don't know when this revelation came to me, but I ended up going from worried, anxious, impatient, and fearful of being alone to knowing that God will send me the right person at the right time. Even if He has to bring me to him. It's going to happen. The only thing I need to do is rest in God and continue to live a life that pleases Him. God is going to prepare me to be found.

In Genesis 24:1–48, Abraham sends a servant on a mission to find a wife for his son Isaac. His son Isaac could have married any local woman, but Abraham did not want that. The servant traveled outside of town, far away from where they lived, and ended up near a well. He said a prayer and asked God to bring him a woman who would help him and his camels get water. That's how he would know that the woman would be worthy enough for Isaac. And what do you know, here comes beautiful Rebekah, right on cue. Rebekah was everything the servant prayed to God for and became an answered prayer.

Do you know how amazing and miraculous that has to be to become someone's answered prayer simply by doing the thing you normally do, or being the kind-hearted person you normally are? That's exactly what happened with Rebekah. I'm sure when Rebekah woke up that morning, she didn't put extra spray in her hair. She didn't wear an extra tight or short robe dress. I'm sure she didn't put on makeup or wear her sparkly sandals. She didn't say, "I need to go to where all the men work in the field to be seen." Rebekah simply went out to fetch some water, as I'm sure she normally did every day. Only this time, God brought this person to her.

I've always heard women say that when they finally stopped looking for and worrying about a partner, that is when their partner showed up. So there has to be some truth to you simply focusing on living your life and trusting the Lord's timing. The story of Rebekah was a clear example of how God will place you exactly where you need to be in order to be found. He will mold you and use your circumstances for your good.

Ladies, I'm here to tell you that the man that God created for you will come find you, and you won't have to do anything extra but live a life that is pleasing to the Lord. You should be healing and growing. You should be working to let go of all the things that are holding you back. You should be allowing God to work on your mind and heart. Allow Him to prepare you to be found. Allow Him to prepare you to be someone's answered prayer.

SINGLES WHO FLOURISH (NOTE 7)
APRIL 25, 2023
Annette Visions

The other day I was scrolling on social media, and I came across this guy who made a video talking about how he decided to change his life for his wife. I don't remember what was said verbatim, but I specifically remember this gentleman talking about how he made the choice to be the best version of himself because this woman, whom he fell madly in love with, deserved that.

Do you want to know how he became the best version of himself? He said he turned to God. He gave his life to the Lord and allowed Him to change him from the inside out. I sat and watched this six-minute clip in awe. Like, how amazing and great is it for someone to love another so much that they are willing to make a drastic change to benefit that other person? God, I see what you have done for others! Lol. But seriously, from what this gentleman described, this was one of the best decisions he ever made for himself.

We complain so much about the dating pool and this generation of singles. A lot of people are either playing games or don't really know what they want. For you to find someone who is willing to do the work and turn to God for help to become better for you is so moving. I feel like that's one of the highest forms of love. Also, knowing that God is so powerful and transformational is amazing to me. My mentor once told me that most people don't even know their full personality or potential because of fear. Fear has definitely held me back for a long time, but it wasn't until I gave my heart to God that He stepped in and changed everything. I am no longer afraid.

I know that what God has for me is for me only. I know that God is transforming me and my person to be who He has created us to be. I know that the only way I will make it through anything is if I continue to keep the faith and know that I am covered. I don't have to figure anything out. Nor do I have to do anything extra but continue to heal, grow, and flourish in Christ. After all, He is my help!

SINGLES WHO FLOURISH (NOTE 8)
APRIL 27, 2023

Annette Visions

"I love you, Annette. You are beautiful and smart. You are blessed and highly favored. Royal blood flows through your veins. You are marvelously and wonderfully made. Today will be a great day. Great news is coming. New doors are opening. God is blessing you with elevated blessings. Wherever God places you, you will flourish!"

Yesterday, as I was standing in front of the mirror repeating the same declaration that I say to myself every morning after I get out of the shower, I realized how far God has brought me. For me to be able to say this declaration with confidence, while admiring my reflection in the mirror, is a major accomplishment. If I told you that I did not always like what I saw when I looked in the mirror, would you have believed me? Well, believe it or not, I did not.

Throughout my life, I've always been complimented on my looks. But I never saw what outsiders saw. I struggled with low self-esteem for a while, and it reflected a lot in my decisions, especially when it came to relationships. I think a lot of women can relate. At one point or another, maybe you were free, confident, or thriving, and then you met someone or ran into a situation that just completely broke you down. It took you out of your element and took away that spark. And in doing so, your insecurities made you start gravitating toward people and things that were not so great because that is what made you feel better about yourself.

Yes, this has happened to me in my past, but one thing I do know: God did not hold it against me, and He got me through it. He is still getting me through it. Now, I want to tell you that it was easy for me to move forward from, but I would be lying if I said that. This took work. Work on my part. Physical work. Mental work. Financial work. Emotional work. Spiritual work. It wasn't until I fully surrendered to God that I really started to see a turnaround in the way that I viewed myself.

Yes, you should lean on God to help you and heal you, but you also need to meet Him halfway. You must be willing to do the work. When I say "work," I mean taking the first step by releasing all the things, people, and places that you know are not right for you. Here are some more steps to help you see yourself the way God sees you:

1. Anyone or anything that does not make you feel good about yourself should be released.

2. Come up with a declaration to declare to yourself in the mirror daily until you really start to embody the words. You can even use the one I listed above.

3. Continue to get close to God. Read your Bible and study His word. This way, when doubt starts to fill your mind, you can remind yourself through Scripture of who you are by using God's exact words.

4. Lastly, ask God for help. If you need someone, He is there 24/7 to listen and give you whatever you need. He loves you and wants the best for you. There isn't anyone more reliable.

Ladies, I want to remind you to start seeing yourselves the way that God sees you. He created you, so He knows who you are. He knows what you are capable of. He knows who you belong to. You are a masterpiece. God's greatest creation. Those insecurities mean nothing to Him. You were marvelously and wonderfully made. It's time that you start seeing this whenever you look in the mirror.

> "For You formed my innermost parts; You knit me [together] in my mother's womb. I will give thanks and praise to You, for I am fearfully and wonderfully made; Wonderful

are Your works, And my soul knows it very well." (Psalm 139:13–14, AMP)

SINGLES WHO FLOURISH (NOTE 9)

MAY 1, 2023

Annette Visions

I finally did something that I have not done in a very long time. It was something so simple, and yet uncommon for me to do. I finally lifted my head up to look at the sky.

I know what you're thinking: "That's no big deal, right?" Wrong. It wasn't until this moment that I finally realized how I much I didn't take the time to appreciate God's creation.

Let me clarify. I am 100% that woman who enjoys seeing and experiencing beautiful things. I love going to different art galleries and visiting different museum exhibits. I love going to see plays and opera concerts. And yet, I never took out the time to appreciate the artwork that's right in front of me. The artwork that I can see for free daily. The work of the greatest painter yet, God.

Genesis 1:1–14 talks about how God created one of His many masterpieces. It shows how He created the heavens and the earth. This was before He created man. Now, being a person who studies the Bible, you would think that I would be keen to examine these exhibits, but no.

If you're anything like me, your head is down most of the day due to any one of the many technology devices that they have created to keep our minds and eyes distracted. Also, being very determined and motivated to elevate my career has made me spend most of my time in an office glued to a computer screen. But all of that ended as soon as I lifted my head. Staring at the clouds for five minutes was all the reminder that I needed.

One of my main goals is to get better at appreciating the here and now. I plan to get better at appreciating who and what is around me. My goal is to travel around the world to see all of God's many great exhibits. The mountains, the hills, the forests, the rivers, the lakes, the valleys, the desert. All major and minor views. Just knowing that God created this world within seven days is what makes each exhibit as important as the next.

I think in order for me to appreciate God creating my "Adam," I need to appreciate all that was here before him. I'm hoping that my "Adam" is the type who appreciates it as well, because hopefully we can experience these exhibits around the world together. All while serving God. What do you think? Is this a good idea?

SINGLES WHO FLOURISH (NOTE 10)

MAY 4, 2023

Annette Visions

Today I want to do something different. I want to pray for anyone who is struggling in their singleness season. Praying always helps me, so I'm hoping it will help you. Maybe you are going through a storm right now, maybe you are feeling defeated, or maybe you are just giving up hope. I want you to know that God has not forgotten you and He is right there, so keep holding on.

Father, I ask that you wrap your loving arms around whoever is reading this right now. God, I ask that you send a peace that passes all understanding, including our own. God, I pray that you bring us patience and faith unlike anything we have ever experienced. God, help us to live lives that are pleasing to you. Whenever we grow weary, drown us with renewed strength. Give us clarity in the direction You want us to go. Send your angels to surround and protect us. Continue to heal our hearts and minds. Bring the right people, opportunities, and connections. Help us to release all the people, places, and things that are not right for us. Open the right doors and keep the wrong doors shut. God, only You know what is next for us, and only You know what is best for us. Help us to fully trust in You and Your timing.

In Jesus's mighty name we pray. Amen.

SINGLES WHO FLOURISH (NOTE 11)
MAY 9, 2023
Annette Visions

I'm going to share a story of when I was younger and not that financially responsible. Please don't hold this against me.

I remember years ago when I needed a place to stay and my credit was not in a great place. I kept getting denied for the places that I applied to live. At one point, I even stopped applying because I was afraid of being rejected again. This was a really tough time in my life, and I didn't know how I would weather this storm.

I recently read Matthew 8:23–26, when Jesus and his disciples were on a boat and a storm came. All the followers were afraid of drowning, and yet Jesus was sleeping. Can you believe that during this storm, Jesus was knocked out?

I can only imagine the boat rocking back and forth, hard. You can hear the loud thunder and feel the water splashing in the boat, and yet Jesus was peacefully sleeping. That tells me that Jesus knew something that we all didn't know. All He needed to do was rebuke the winds and sea, and everything stopped.

Anytime I catch myself in a storm and I begin to get anxious or worried, I imagine Jesus sleeping through it peacefully. I remind myself how easy it was for Jesus to calm the storm. Because if He did it for them, He will definitely do it for me. I remind myself that if Jesus is not worried about it, then why should I be? That's when my faith is fully ignited.

As time went on during my quest for an apartment, I decided to work on my credit and my faith to get both in a better spot. I remember showering one day and just talking to Jesus, but this talk was different. I felt myself throwing in the towel of trying to handle this situation of finding a place on my own. I gave it all to Jesus that day in the shower. I kid you not, a few days later I applied for a nice luxury apartment in faith. Then I got the call that not only was I approved, but I didn't even need to put down a deposit because my credit was good. I also was able to get the apartment that I wanted for a cheaper price two days before I was set to move in. I knew it was Jesus. He woke up and calmed the storm.

I want to remind you that if you are facing any storms

right now, do not be afraid. I just showed you two examples of how Jesus calmed storms. So you should know it's not impossible. Although the boat may be rocky and the winds may be brutal, you should be able to rest well knowing that the Lord can calm the storm in the blink of an eye. It may take faith and patience on your part to weather the storm, but Jesus will step in to calm it.

> *"Jesus got into a boat, and his followers went with him. After the boat left the shore, a very bad storm began on the lake. The waves covered the boat. But Jesus was sleeping. The followers went to him and woke him. They said, 'Lord, save us! We will drown!' Jesus answered, 'Why are you afraid? You don't have enough faith.' Then he stood up and gave a command to the wind and the water. The wind stopped, and the lake became very calm." (Matthew 8:23–26, ERV)*

SINGLES WHO FLOURISH (NOTE 12)

MAY 11, 2023

Annette Visions

Confession: One of the biggest things that I have struggled with is not asking for help. In my past, I felt like I had to do everything on my own. I felt like I never really had anyone that I could count on to help me. I mean, I had people in my life, like family and friends, but I never felt comfortable enough to reach out to them for help. Crazy, right? Some of this stemmed from personal feelings, and then some stemmed from personal experience. In the past, people did not show up for me when and how I needed them to, so I just learned to not even bother to ask for help.

It's funny that going through my singleness journey shined a light on this "me vs. the world" way of thinking. I was really convincing myself that I had to handle everything alone. I felt like there was no one I could turn to. No one who would understand. If I asked for help, I would be judged. I would be talked about. I would be degraded. I would be looked at as "weak." But here's some reality: I was not Superwoman. I was not obligated to carry the weight of the world on my shoulders.

If you have ever struggled with not asking for help or experienced doing everything yourself, you will quickly learn that this won't work once you're in a relationship. Your partner will know when you're mad, sad, happy, or preoccupied. They are connected to you, so even if you don't show it, they can feel it in the connection. You will now have someone that you can trust and know that they will show up for you every time. Sometimes without you even having to ask. Because this is what real love is. So why wouldn't you allow them to help you?

Now here's something that I want to leave you with: struggling in silence is never the answer. I had to learn the hard way, and I want to encourage you to not follow in my footsteps. If you are experiencing this, make today the last day. Ask for help! If you feel invisible, insecure, unlovable, forgotten, or too far gone to be helped, don't allow that to stop you. We all live and learn, but please learn to seek out help if you need it. No matter what kind of help you need.

I'm sure you know what I'm going to say, but the best person to always seek out for help, who is guaranteed to show up for you every time, is God. Go to Him. Lean on Him. Trust in Him. He sees you. He hears you. He loves you. He has not forgotten you!

> *"But the Lord says, 'Can a woman forget her baby? Can she forget the child who came from her body? Even if she can forget her children, I cannot forget you.'" (Isaiah 49:15, ERV)*

SINGLES WHO FLOURISH (NOTE 13)

MAY 16, 2023

Annette Visions

One of the many reasons why I love to remind you that God has not forgotten you is because for years I have felt forgotten. For some strange reason, I made myself believe that I was unimportant, invisible, and unworthy of love. Especially God's love. Between taking part in bad relationships and friendships and completely turning my back on God at one point, this led me to believe that God didn't want to have anything to do with me.

That feeling of unworthiness led me to question God. Not about Him, but about me. "Why me?" I caught myself asking God again yesterday. "Why do you favor me? Why have you chosen me? Why have you held on to me? I'm flawed. I'm not the best writer. I'm not the best speaker. I don't have that much experience. I'm not the best prayer warrior. I'm not the best when it comes to studying my Bible. I do okay. I'm not the model Christian. I have made and continue to make mistakes. Why is it me?" I caught myself asking God this more and more as it was evident that He has been sending reinforcements to help guide my path to what is next.

After asking God this, I randomly opened my Bible later that night before bed, and I was led to read Deuteronomy 6:1–18. This passage showed how Moses explained to the freed Israelites what it meant to love and serve God. He explained all of God's commands, rules, and regulations. God expected a wholehearted commitment and holiness from the Israelites after being freed from Pharaoh's reign. But these verses aren't what got me; it was Deuteronomy 7:7–8 that stood out to me:

> *"The Lord did not set his heart on you and choose you because you were more numerous than other nations, for you were the smallest of all nations! Rather, it was simply that the Lord loves you, and he was keeping the oath he had sworn to your ancestors. That is why the Lord rescued you with such a strong hand from your slavery and from the oppressive hand of Pharaoh, king of Egypt." (Deuteronomy 7:7–8, NLT)*

God gave me my answer. My soul felt like it was being wiped clean with every tear that fell down my face after reading these verses. It wasn't because of what I did right or what I did wrong in my life; it was simply because He loves me. God chose me because of His love. He knows what He is capable of through me. It is He who qualifies me. No strings. No ulterior motives. No conditions. He loves me. He freed me from my past sins and gave me new life. He made sure that everything from the beginning of my life to the end is in place to allow me to fulfill His will.

I'm telling you this because I want you to know two things:

1. No sin or trouble is too hard or too terrible for God to save you from. God will part seas and cause the earth to shake in order to rescue and protect you. We saw this with Moses and the freed Israelites slaves who escaped Pharaoh.

2. If God chose you, He will qualify you. This means that everything that you need in order to fulfill His purpose will be provided without you having to ask. From beginning to end. God mapped it out already. God chose Moses to lead His people out of Egypt to freedom, and this plan was set in motion from the time Moses was born.

Maybe you're asking God the same questions: "God, why me? Why did I have to experience those horrible breakups? Why didn't he/she want me? Why have I been single for a long time? Why don't I ever connect with anyone? Why can't I catch a break? Why did you choose me and not my friends or family?" Trust me, God knows what He's doing.

God has a purpose for your life that He needs for you to fulfill. Those things or people that you wanted might have interfered with God's plan. They could have destroyed you. The only person who knows is God. All you need to do is ask God to help you live a life that is aligned to His will. That means that God chooses the who, what, where, when, why, and how. Will you trust His plan and His love?

SINGLES WHO FLOURISH (NOTE 14)
MAY 18, 2023
Annette Visions

I would like to pray again, but this prayer will be for a season of openness. That is my prayer for myself, for you, for anyone who is struggling with being open to God, to love, to faith, to healing, to wisdom, to knowledge, to understanding, to change, to discipline. Just know that whatever is taking place in your life right now, God will open you up to a new level of strength and will see you through it.

God, I come to you today to first give thanks for whoever is reading this right now. God, I thank You that You allowed for them to wake up to see another blessed day in their right frame of mind.

And Lord, I come to You today to ask that You usher

us in to a season of openness. Lord, open our mouths so that we may continuously bless Your Holy name. Open our hearts and minds to purity. Remove all the things that are not of You and replace them with Your greatness. Open our spiritual eyes and ears so that we may see Your vision for our future and hear Your direction, as our steps are being ordered. Lord, if there is anyone who is struggling with faith or with opening their heart to love, Your love, remove the barriers and blockages. Drown us in Your love and embrace.

You said that You would open up the windows of Heaven and pour out blessings for us. So Lord, if there are any blessings that are being held up, open those windows, doors, and opportunities. Prepare us to receive all that You have already written our names on. It may not look like things are happening in the physical, but Lord, I know that You are moving in the spiritual. Thank You for it all!

In Your precious name we pray, Amen.

SINGLES WHO FLOURISH (NOTE 15)
MAY 25, 2023
Annette Visions

    I think two of the main things we look for while we are single and dating are comfort and security. We just want to feel safe and secure. We want to feel comfortable. In my personal opinion, comfort should be the bare minimum. Who wants to be around someone and not feel comfortable with them? Comfort leads to trust, or shall I say, trust leads to comfort.

    For a long time, I was looking for the man who will give me this feeling. Just being around him would make me feel like I can just sit back and relax. I could be my authentic self. Like I didn't have to worry about anything because I knew that I would always be safe and feel taken care of when I was with him. That's what I wanted. I mean, I still want that and plan on having that, but not in the way that you think.

I realized that I may be looking for something that another person was not supposed to "give" me. Maybe I'm holding people to too high a standard. People are people and can only give someone what they were taught or have to give. Maybe looking for comfort from someone else is not the best thing. Maybe the comfort and security I am looking for have been in me all along. You want to know why? God is my comfort and security. He lives in me. Maybe the person I have been looking for is God.

> "You can go to him for protection. He will cover you like a bird spreading its wings over its babies. You can trust him to surround and protect you like a shield." (Psalm 91:4, ERV)

God reminds us throughout the Bible how He will always protect and provide comfort. God reassures us not to be afraid because even in the darkest of times, He will be there. Now, I'm not saying that having a partner who can protect me and always ensure that I am comfortable is impossible. God can and will bless you with a person exactly like this! I am saying that I do not need this from any other person because God already has this covered. And this is something that I can always count on. No doubt about it!

> "Even if I walk through a valley as dark as the grave, I will not be afraid of any danger, because you are with me. Your rod and staff comfort me." (Psalm 23:4, ERV)

SINGLES WHO FLOURISH (NOTE 16)

MAY 30, 2023

Annette Visions

I used to imagine myself just lying in bed all day. In a comfortable bed with the softest sheets and the best thread count, on the fluffiest comforter set. White sheets, white walls, white curtains, with the softest cream carpet, a fresh bouquet of flowers on my nightstand, and a bunch of pictures scattered on my shelves of all the people I love. I don't even need to be sleeping in the bed. I'm just doing nothing but relaxing.

If your life is anything like mine, you are on the go constantly. I'm up at 5 a.m. and back home in bed sometimes by 10 p.m. The hours in between are spent working nonstop to assist whomever I can to make their lives run smoothly. I desperately need a break. But somehow I feel guilty for wanting a break.

I remember when I was younger, I thought I would run a successful business while being an amazing wife and mother. That was my plan. I wanted to do it all. I wanted to be Superwoman. Taking care of everything and everyone. Winning at all things. But as of late, I am seriously rethinking this plan.

What changed? For years, I have been relying on my own talents, gifts, abilities, and strength to get me through. I think I'm experiencing what they call "burnout." Silly of me to think that I could do all of this on my own. Well, the reality is I cannot do this on my own. I so desperately need the Lord. I have been trying to make my plan work instead of trusting in the plan that the Lord has for me.

> *"'For I know the plans I have for you,' says the Lord. 'They are plans for good and not for disaster, to give you a future and a hope.'"* (Jeremiah 29:11, NLT)

I had a long talk with God this month and asked Him to step in and assist me in my life. I realized that I am nothing without Him. I cannot accomplish anything without Him. So I'm not going to try anymore. I won't say that I will completely give up my plan of running a successful business while being a great wife and mother, but what I will say is that I am going to allow God to take over. Doing things my way has led me to feeling overwhelmed and tired, so I'm sure God's plan for my life is way better than my own.

How about you? Have you been burning yourself out

trying to make your plans work, or have you been trusting in the Lord's plan for your life?

SINGLES WHO FLOURISH (NOTE 17)

JUNE 1, 2023

Annette Visions

"I will bless the LORD at all times: his praise shall continually be in my mouth." (Psalm 34:1, KJV)

This scripture means so much more to me now than it did a few years ago. You know what changed? Experience.

I have been through a lot, but that doesn't stop my praise for the Lord. I've realized that it's easy to praise Him when things are going great. When everything is working out. When you see the blessings, you feel great and are willing to give thanks to God. But what happens when things aren't going so great? What happens when you don't see any progress? What happens when that prayer request goes unanswered or you feel it is taking too long to come to pass? Will you still praise the Lord?

I am here to encourage and remind you to continuously praise the Lord like it says in the Scripture. That means that you should never stop. No matter what you see or don't see. No matter what happens or doesn't happen. This continuous praise is known to be a life changer. It's known to be a heart changer. It's known to be a mindset changer. So I ask that you try it for yourself.

SINGLES WHO FLOURISH (NOTE 18)

JUNE 29, 2023

Annette Visions

Have you ever been to a wedding and heard 1 Corinthians 13:4–7? There's a reason that this passage is widely used at weddings. This passage explains the basis of love. It tells you how to love and what love looks like. This passage sets the blueprint for all unions.

I know what you're thinking: "Why are you bringing up love and marriage if you are talking to singles?" Well, the answer to this is simple: Love has no bounds. Love is unbiased. Love should be well established before we ever get into any relationship or union.

> "Love is patient and kind. Love is not jealous or boastful or proud or rude. It does not demand its own way. It is not irritable, and it keeps no record of being wronged. It does not

> *rejoice about injustice but rejoices whenever the truth wins out. Love never gives up, never loses faith, is always hopeful, and endures through every circumstance." (1 Corinthians 13:4–7, NLT)*

This passage gives a description of how love should look for yourself, for God, and for others. I was taught growing up that God is love. God is the One Who determines what love is. He tells us how love should look. You cannot have one without the other: "But anyone who does not love does not know God, for God is love" (1 John 4:8, NLT). That's why it is important that you have a union with God before having a union with another.

God can show you what it means to love and be loved. God can show you how to love yourself. God can show you how to love another. There's a reason that love is talked about a lot throughout the Bible. It is very important. One of the greatest feelings. I want to encourage you to allow God to show you what love is. You can do this by allowing Him into your heart.

> "Three things will last forever—faith, hope, and love—and the greatest of these is love."
> (1 Corinthians 13:13, NLT)

SINGLES WHO FLOURISH (NOTE 19)

JULY 12, 2023

Annette Visions

During my Bible study this week, I read Luke 8:43–48, which talked about the story of the woman with the issue of blood. This woman bled constantly for twelve years, and nothing she did or found would cure it. This woman was in desperate need for a miracle and decided that Jesus was the only one who could heal her. She was so desperate that all she could lean on was her faith. Her faith is what made her decide that just touching a piece of Jesus's clothing would be enough to heal her.

Have you ever been there? Have you ever been in desperate need of a miracle? Have you ever had a bad breakup or been in a state where you felt like nothing or no one could help you but Jesus? Well, I'm here to tell you that just like with the woman with the issue of blood, a touch in faith will work. A touch in faith can heal you.

Yes, it's that easy. Reach out and touch Jesus. You can ask Him for what you need. You can open your heart and allow Him in. That heartbreak that you have been carrying around for years, Jesus can heal with a touch. The guilt and shame that you have had to endure, Jesus can cure with a touch. In that storm that you are trying to weather, Jesus can protect you with a touch.

Now, I don't know about you, but one of my favorite love languages is physical touch. Whenever I am around people, I love to be affectionate. Whether I am holding hands, embracing them, or just staying in close proximity. That's my way of showing and receiving love. But Jesus is so supernatural that you don't even need to touch his body or skin in order to feel His love or receive His healing power. His clothing will do. Reach out for Jesus. Give Him a touch in faith. Know that whatever you are believing in Him for will be done!

> *"A woman in the crowd had suffered for twelve years with constant bleeding, and she could find no cure. Coming up behind Jesus, she touched the fringe of his robe. Immediately, the bleeding stopped. 'Who touched me?' Jesus asked. Everyone denied it, and Peter said, 'Master, this whole crowd is pressing up against you.' But Jesus said, 'Someone deliberately touched me, for I felt healing power go out from me.' When the woman*

realized that she could not stay hidden, she began to tremble and fell to her knees in front of him. The whole crowd heard her explain why she had touched him and that she had been immediately healed. 'Daughter,' he said to her, 'your faith has made you well. Go in peace.'" (Luke 8:43–48, NLT)

SINGLES WHO FLOURISH (NOTE 20)

JULY 25, 2023

Annette Visions

First, let me apologize for my absence. This past week was really tough for me. It started off great with me spending time with the Lord, and then it just seemed like I was fighting to make it through the remainder of the week.

I have been attending church more regularly, and one Sunday I heard the preacher ask the congregation if we had faith that God can do it. But that wasn't what floored me. What floored me was his next question: "Do you have faith that God can do it *for you?*" That is what I needed to hear. Everything started to make sense.

I don't know if you can relate to when you are believing in God for something and it seems like it is taking forever. Maybe you see other people receiving their blessings, and you're wondering, "What is the holdup with my blessings?" (I'm just being real here.) You begin to question if it will happen for you. I have been there, and it wasn't until the preacher asked that question that I realized that my faith was being affected by my impatience and my way of thinking.

Because of the delay. Because of the uncertainty. Because I had to witness others around me receiving. I was losing my faith that God would do it for me. However, do you want to know how I was able to strengthen my faith? By remembering what God did for others and knowing that I am no different.

I am no different from Esther or Ruth. I am no different from Daniel or David. Think about someone you personally know who just received a major breakthrough or blessing. You are no different from them. God loves us all the same, and if He did it for them, He can do it for you.

But just remember, whatever it is that you are asking or believing for needs to be aligned with God's will for your life. It needs to be what God wants for you. And this is the part you have to come to terms with. Faith is letting go and letting God handle it. Can your faith withstand it if God does not give you what you're believing in Him for? Will you lose faith in God?

Ask yourself these questions and answer them honestly. This is what helped me to strengthen my faith. I hope it helps to strengthen yours also.

"Now faith is the substance of things hoped for, the evidence of things not seen." (Hebrews)

SINGLES WHO FLOURISH (NOTE 21)

AUGUST 2, 2023

Annette Visions

So this may be my final note regarding this singleness journey. I don't want to say that I'm giving up, but I do feel like I would be better off surrendering everything to God.

> "The steps of a good man are ordered by the LORD: And he delighteth in his way. Though he fall, he shall not be utterly cast down: For the LORD upholdeth him with his hand." (Psalm 37:23–24, KJV)

The Bible tells us that God will order your steps. And if you trust Him, if you truly believe that He has your best interest at heart, then you should allow Him to lead the way.

> "Yea, though I walk through the valley of

> *the shadow of death, I will fear no evil: for thou art with me; Thy rod and thy staff they comfort me." (Psalm 23:4, KJV)*

I trust that wherever this path is leading me to will ultimately be in the presence of the Lord, whether I'm single or in a relationship. Changing my relationship status is no longer the goal. Getting married is no longer the goal. Of course, I would love that, but I would rather pursue the will of the Lord. The ultimate goal is to be aligned with Him. And it is in Him that I will trust and love forever.

I pray that your journey also leads you into the arms of the Lord. I pray that you'll give your heart to Him. He loves you more than you can ever imagine.

> *"Trust in him at all times; ye people, Pour out your heart before him: God is a refuge for us. Selah." (Psalm 62:8, KJV)*

CONCLUSION

If you're reading this, that means that you made it through this twenty-one-day devotional. I pray that these notes blessed you while reading them, just as much as it did for me writing them. When I first started writing these notes, I did not know what to expect. What I did know was that I needed a change in my singleness season. I knew that I wanted to get closer to the Lord, and the only way to do that was through His word and prayer. I needed to develop an intimate relationship with Christ.

As I was growing closer to the Lord, I wanted to honor Him in any way that I could. The only way to honor the Lord is to share what I have learned with you. I pray that this devotional helps you to heal, grow, and flourish with the Lord. James 4:8 (KJV) says, "Draw nigh to God, and he will draw nigh to you. Cleanse your hands, ye sinners; and purify your hearts, ye double minded." You must be committed to your healing journey. Go all in. You can't be indecisive. Give it all to the Lord.

Here are some questions for you to answer in your journal. Really take time to think your answers through so you can bring them to the Lord. In order for you to have an intimate relationship with Him, you have to be real and honest with Him.

1. What are a few takeaways from this devotional?

2. Have any of the notes resonated with you more strongly than the others? If so, why?

3. Is there any story or person in the Bible that you feel reflects your life at this current moment?

4. Are there any areas in your life that you feel that you need to allow God to handle?

5. Do you believe that God knows who you are and loves you?

6. Do you believe that God will bless you with your heart's desires, or do you have doubts?

7. Have you ever experienced heartbreak before? If so, how did you get past it?

8. Will you trust the Lord with your heart?

I want to leave you with this: God loves you more than you know. You are His first love. He loved you so much that He sacrificed His only son for you and me: "For this is how God loved the world: He gave his one and only Son, so that everyone who believes in him will not perish but have eternal life" (John 3:16, NLT). Don't ever forget that. He is waiting to have a relationship with you. All you need to do is open your heart and allow Him in to handle the rest.

POSTSCRIPT

You are now part of my community. In this community we love one another. We hold each other accountable. We pray for one another. We keep each other encouraged. But most importantly, we water each other so that we can heal, grow, and flourish in love, life, and the Lord. I pray that God continues to heal your heart and mind.

You can visit me at **www.annettecornell.com** and/or email me at **support@annettecornell.com**. Be sure to add "SWF" to the subject line of your email. I would love to hear from you.

SCRIPTURE INDEX

Romans 8:39, KJV – Intro

Romans 5:8, NLT – Intro

Psalm 84:11, NLT – Note 1

Song of Songs 8:4, NLT – Note 2

Genesis 2:21–22, KJV – Note 2

Proverbs 31:10–31 – Note 3

Philippians 1:6, NLT – Note 4

John 3:16, NLT – Note 5

Genesis 24:1–48 – Note 6

Psalm 139:13–14, AMP – Note 8

Matthew 8:23–26, ERV – Note 11

Isaiah 49:15, ERV – Note 12

Deuteronomy 6:1–18 – Note 13

Deuteronomy 7:7–8, NLT – Note 13

Psalm 91:4, ERV – Note 15

Psalm 23:4, ERV – Note 15

Jeremiah 29:11, NLT – Note 16

Psalm 34:1, KJV – Note 17

1 Corinthians 13:4–7, NLT – Note 18

1 John 4:8, NLT – Note 18

1 Corinthians 13:13, NLT – Note 18

Luke 8:43–48, NLT – Note 19
Hebrews 11:1, KJV – Note 20
Psalm 37:23–24, KJV – Note 21
Psalm 23:4, KJV – Note 21
Psalm 62:8, KJV – Note 21
John 3:16, NLT – Conclusion

Printed in the USA
CPSIA information can be obtained
at www.ICGtesting.com
LVHW020726210624
783605LV00007B/128